REVENUE PLAYBOOK

Applying the Simple Rules of Hotel Revenue Management

Johan Hammer

Johan@revenuesuperstar.com
Instagram: revenuesuperstar
revenuesuperstar.com/newsletter

ISBN 978-15-482-5579-4

About Johan Hammer

I have more than 10 years experience in the hospitality industry, including 6+ years of revenue management experience.

In 2015, I earned a certificate from Cornell University after completing their course titled, *Advanced Hospitality Revenue Management: Pricing and Demand Strategies*.

Most recently, in June 2017, I co-founded a travel startup called Instaroom.travel where we build cool messaging technology to help hotels digitalize guest conversations and convert complicated bookings directly on their own websites. Our technology is 100% AI ready, which means it contains many smart tools and the ability to automate most conversations. The hotel website is the most visited department in a hotel, and currently it's unstaffed. The first step a hotel should take is to put a messaging widget on their website. Messaging is here to stay. After all, research shows that at least 88% of people born after 1981 prefer communicating via messaging.

Feel free to reach out to me at johan@instaroom.travel to learn more and to get a free trial of Instaroom.travel for your hotel or brand. www.instaroom.travel

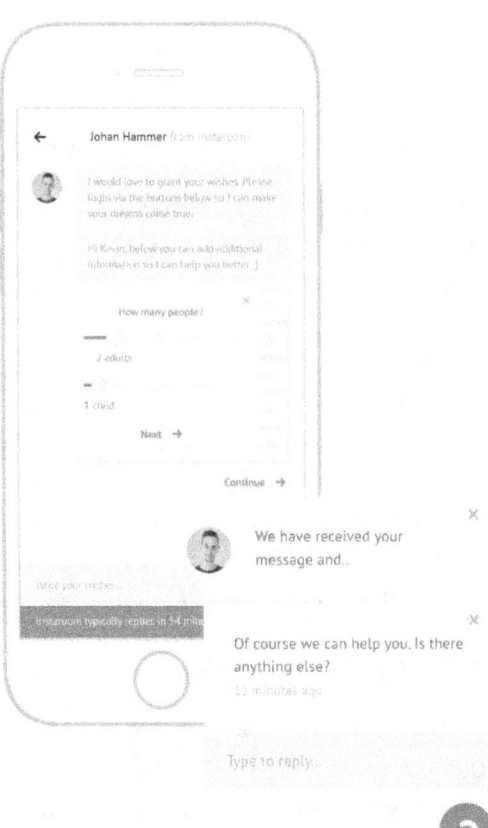

My previous endeavor was as a Revenue & Distribution Specialist for a large Scandinavian hotel chain, First Hotels. My main role there was to consult with our hotels regarding revenue- and distribution-related matters. I also internally analyzed and suggested new strategies for the brand and its stakeholders.

Table of Contents

Introduction and How to Use This Book

This book should be used as a tool to help you manage your daily challenges as a revenue manager. While we have many digital tools at our disposal nowadays, this more basic "old-school" approach will help you to manage the entirety of your digital world by providing you with a comprehensive helicopter-view perspective of your practice as a hotel revenue manager.

Use it every day. Bring it with you to hotel revenue meetings. Or bring it home with you over the weekend to plan the week ahead. Use it to highlight pricing decisions and competitor movements.

In the first part of this book, we will explore what every playbook should help you focus your daily activities on and why, and tie these ideas to some "best practice" revenue management guidelines and rules. In the second part of this book, I provide examples of the journal pages that every revenue manager's playbook should include, and explain how you can use them efficiently and effectively on the job. In addition to the multiple copies of each journal page provided in this book, you can download PDF versions of these pages at www.revenuesuperstar.com/playbook.

When reading this book, remember that using a playbook can help you manage the revenue of either a single hotel or a cluster of hotels.

Use a playbook to:
- Keep track of daily pricing activities and strategies
- Note the best takeaways from each day
- Maintain an action list
- Plan your day to maximize outputs

- Assist with forecasting
- Take notes during revenue meetings
- Highlight trends
- Track your promotions and campaigns

Think of *The Revenue Superstar Playbook* as the personal assistant that will help you stay organized in a noisy digital world.

Earlier in my own career, I worked with journal pages similar to the ones I have included as examples in this book. I used them every day, but never in such an organized manner as what I have laid out here. A playbook is something I wish I had available to me back when I managed the revenue for multiple hotels.

This, in short, is the playbook for the modern revenue manager.

If you have already read my previous book, *Revenue Superstar! The Simple Rules of Hotel Revenue Management*, you will recognize some of the ideas I present in the *Advice and Guidelines* section that follows. Nevertheless, I recommend that you still read through these pages because they will provide you with a blueprint for working with this playbook in the best way possible.

As you are reading, please refer to the glossary of terms if you encounter any industry lingo pertaining to hotel revenue management for which you are unfamiliar.

Before we begin. Make sure to sign up for my newsletter. Be the first one to know when there is news updates or special promotions.

revenuesuperstar.com/newsletter

Part 1: Advice and Guidelines

Which Numbers Are Important?

First, let's review some important numbers and KPIs.

Not all KPIs, and numbers (the data) in general, are equally important. This probably does not come as a surprise to you, but you may still wonder what numbers are actually important enough to measure on a daily and weekly basis? The numbers that you will want to focus upon are the ones that give you enough actionable insights to help you optimize your hotel's revenue streams.

To determine which numbers you should utilize most regularly, apply the Triple-A rule. Think of the numbers that meet the requirements of the Triple-A rule this way:

-   They must be **Actionable**
    The data should provide clear direction for strategic and managerial decisions.
-   They must be **Accessible**
    The data should be simple to find and simple to read.
-   They must be **Auditable**
    The data must be real in the sense that it is derived from clean and accurate data sources.

Obviously, the numbers you choose will very much be connected to your overarching revenue-management strategy.

My highly biased recommendation, however, is to monitor the following KPIs very closely, as each has a strong correlation with higher hotel profitability. Furthermore, each of these KPIs is universal, and thus probably hold true for most hotels. They include:

- Hotel satisfaction score
- Pickup (often confused with pace)
- Booking pace

Reputation Management

Let's briefly review Reputation Management, as it will provide us with enough information to test the Triple-A rule on the hotel satisfaction score.

Studies from www.reviewpro.com demonstrate that the top three reasons why a guest selects a hotel are:

- Guest experience factors (i.e., guest reviews and satisfaction scores)
- Location
- Price

With this in mind, it is easy to understand why the guest experience factor plays such a big role in the ranking algorithms of various websites. It also explains why reputation management is becoming increasingly important and is an accurate predictor of a hotel's performance.

Do you know what your guests are saying about your hotel? Do you reply to online reviews? What is your online reputation?

We can all agree that a high hotel satisfaction score and positive reviews are important, but we also know that it is very time consuming to read and reply to online reviews.

Luckily, there are many systems out there that can gather all this review data for you. These systems can generate important KPIs and even competitive comparisons, which can help you to determine the correct value of your product. Such measurements can also help you understand how to best price yourself in the market. Most systems even allow you to dive deeper into the data to see which departments currently drive negative feedback. You can then quickly identify the source of negative feedback and set up the actions necessary to make improvements.

The ability to read and reply to online reviews and comments on social media through a simple user interface is another key feature, and one of the main reasons for investing in a good reputation management system in the first place. Moreover, with a good Rep system, you can also drill down to see what aspect or which department is underperforming.

Reputation management is where hotel operation meets revenue management and where accurate insights can lead to increased hotel guest satisfaction and profitability. I think of guest satisfaction scores or reputation management as digital value units. This is because an online hotel satisfaction score and reputation are equal to the perceived value of a hotel. Travelers view them as strong indicators of whether or not they should select a hotel, thus making them good gauges to determine how much the hotel can charge for a room in comparison to what their competitors charge. We'll take a closer look at this in the next chapter where we'll discuss value pricing.

For now, let's test the Triple-A rule on the Hotel Satisfaction Score.

Is it Actionable? Yes, very. With a good system you can drill down to see which department is underperforming. You can, then, on a daily basis, check and measure the exact result of your actions.

Is it Accessible? Yes, very, as well. But you have to invest in a good system to make it accessible.

Is it Auditable? Yes. The data is based on the direct feedback of guests, online reviews and other interactions. This kind of data is very clean and reliable.

Pickup

Pickup statistics can be a good indicator of hotel performance, which is why you should be analyzing them. We will discuss pickup statistics more in the next chapter, but for now, let's look at a short overview of pickup and see if it passes the Triple-A test.

There are several factors to consider when you look at pickup numbers, but first of all: What is a pickup number? When you look at the pickup you are, for example, going over the reservations you sold the day before. If you look at the current month you could check pickup day by day to determine rate changes. You could also use the pickup data to figure out if you need to set up restrictions to avoid days filling up too quickly, which might cause surrounding days to be blocked for guests who want to stay many nights.

So, does pickup pass the Triple-A test?

Is it Actionable? Yes, very. Normally it gives you a very good indication of which days you need to take action on. Sometimes you will need to dig a bit deeper to figure out exactly what type of segments were booked to determine the right strategy to follow moving forward, but nonetheless it's actionable.

Also, if you have a system that can compare how much you sold this year versus the previous year, you will have a good indication of whether your hotel is performing well or not.

Is it Accessible? It should be. If you have a decent PMS or revenue management system, you should be able to easily pick out these numbers. Otherwise, a simple excel spreadsheet on which you deduct yesterday's reservation overview from today's will suffice.

Is it Auditable? Yes, it is. The numbers come directly from the PMS or CRS. As long as the basic structures behind the scenes are in place the number should be highly reliable.

Pace

Looking at the booking pace provides you with a very good indication of whether a certain time period in the future will perform well for your hotel. The pace tells you if you are in line with the same point in time form the previous year, or, if you get more advanced, if you are where you need to be to reach the goals you set for a specific period.

If your hotel has a diverse business mix, it's important to understand the different booking windows per segment or rate class. The booking pace is your helper to find opportunities at the right point in time. Since all segments behave differently and the booking windows can vary widely, understanding and working with booking pace can be crucial for taking action before a window closes.

Pace and pickup will be discussed more in the coming chapters. But first, does booking pace pass the Triple-A test?

Is it Actionable? Yes, it is. The booking pace provides you with a very clear indication of whether you are moving in the right direction.

Is it Accessible? Yes, but it depends, of course, on whether you have a good business intelligence system or RMS system in place. If not, at the very least, you should be able to pull the data from you PMS and arrange it in a spreadsheet.

Is it Auditable? Same as for pickup: Yes, it is. The numbers come directly from the PMS or CRS. As long as the basic structures behind the scenes are in place, the number should be highly reliable.

Daily Pricing Activities

The decisions you must make regarding daily pricing vary significantly from day to day. It can be rather daunting to know where to begin. Here are some tactics I rely upon over and over again to help me make my decisions more easily.

Pickup trends

Do not adjust your pricing and restrictions based on the pickup number alone; instead, we need to see what is driving the pickup to be able to determine if we need to make any adjustments.

Ask yourself: What was booked yesterday? How did it effect the business we already had?

You might want to think twice before raising your rate if you know that you only had pickup in segments with static rates. In this situation, raising your dynamic rates might depress the pickup on your higher yielding rates—including these dynamic rates—entirely.

Is your pickup filling up too quickly from lower-paying segments? If so, consider setting up some restrictions. A couple of times a week you should probably ask yourself what will be going on 4 to 12 months in the future. In particular, while looking ahead, try to identify new trends or trends that are repeating themselves.

Market and Competitors

It is also important to keep an eye on what your competitors are doing. Watching your competitors will let you know when good opportunities exist to increase rates and help you identify trends before you might have otherwise. If you don't already have a tool to track this kind of information, the major OTAs, at the very least, offer free tools, which is better than nothing. Rate Intelligence from Booking.com is just one example.

I have tested many different tools for competitive rate intelligence, and the best one I have encountered so far is OTA Insight (www.otainsight.com). This site offers a very simple tool with a clean user interface. It also provides very accurate demand forecasts for the near future. I always say, once you find a tool that even a general manager likes and wants to use, then you know you've found the right one. OTA Insight is the first such tool I have found that matches this criterion.

Value Pricing

We can also refer to value pricing as your perceived online value. This is the value the online consumer/shopper equates with your hotel.

Parameters to help you measure your perceived value are, for example, guest satisfaction score, likes, management responses and the number of reviews your hotel receives.

The concept of value pricing is to optimize your pricing in relation to how your potential guests perceive your value compared with your competitor's value or with the market.

It's no secret that hotels with high satisfaction scores get more reservations, but it's easy to forget that it can also be a good pricing indicator. If your hotel delivers higher value than your competitors, you should be able to price your hotel higher.

Other aspects that help to improve your perceived value are good placement on various booking websites and good hotel content, images, videos and text. As you well know, good content and favorable review scores help you rank higher on various websites such as Booking.com and Expedia.

With this in mind, it's easy to see how an increased review score can be converted into digital value units since it's directly correlated to your being able to offer higher prices. If you offer increased value compared with your competitors, you should be able to price accordingly.

A 2013 study from Cornell University shows that hotels with a higher review score are able to sell rooms at higher rates and still retain occupancy levels. In fact, hotels are able to increase rates more than 5% if they increase their review score by 1 point on a scale from 1 to 10.
https://www.tripadvisor.com/TripAdvisorInsights/n724/cornell-study-demonstrates-roi-social-media-and-reviews

Inventory Control

Make sure your room inventory is always balanced.

In other words, make sure you have rooms available when they need to be available. If you sold out of your most popular room type, you might want to upgrade or set up overbooking rules in order not to miss out on good opportunities such as long stayers and last-minute premium rate bookers.

If, for example, your standard room category sells out for a Tuesday, you might miss out on guests who have agreements only for that particular room type, but who want to stay several nights in addition to Tuesday.

Group Pricing

When it comes to group pricing, there are two different aspects worth discussing. One aspect is displacement or what I like to call the "What if". The other aspect concerns what constitutes a good rate to offer a group.

A What If analysis requires that you determine how much business you must say "No" to if you accept a group. Basically, you need to look at what business you are expecting for the dates in question and whether the group replaces that business. You must also remember to add in extra revenues you would not have had otherwise with, for example, transient guests (conference room rental, food, etc.).

To make these calculations and answer these questions, conduct a What If analysis. To do so, you can either look at historical data or forecast performance with these specific dates in mind. Remember, you don't always need to reinvent the wheel when you get a new group request that necessitates making a What If analysis. Take time to create a truly practical template that you can use to make this an effortless procedure every single time.

Here's a very simple What If exercise example:

Our imaginary hotel has a capacity of 100. In other words, the hotel can sell 100 rooms per day.

Here is the forecast for the hotel for the same period the group wants to stay. The group request is spread over 3 days and the number of rooms booked peak on the second day.

FORECAST Excluding Group	Day 1	Day 2	Day 3	TOTAL
Forecast Hotel Occupancy	82%	95%	67%	
Forecast Room Nights	82	95	67	
Forecast Average Rate	$ 167	$ 189	$ 174	
Total Revenue	$13 694	$17 955	$11 658	$43 307

Here is the group request:

GROUP DETAILS	Day 1	Day 2	Day 3
Group Request (number of rooms)	25	30	20
Group Rate Per Room	$ 100	$ 100	$ 100
Group Conference Revenue	$ 500	$ 650	$ 500

This is the new forecast if the group is accepted:

New FORECAST With Group	Day 1	Day 2	Day 3	TOTAL
Forecast Hotel Occupancy	100%	100%	87%	
Forecast Room Nights	100	100	87	
Forecast Average Rate	$ 150	$ 162	$ 157	
Total Revenue (+ new conference revenue)	$15 525	$16 880	$14 158	$46 563

RESULT	Day 1	Day 2	Day 3	TOTAL
Variations	$+1 831	$-1 075	$+2 500	$+3 256

Even if the group receives a much lower price per room
compared with the forecasted average price per room, the
calculation turns out to be a positive. The extra conference
revenue is partially to thank for this. In the end, our imaginary
hotel earns $3 256 extra by accepting this group. Please note
that this is an oversimplified example, which does not consider
what reservations are already on the books, the additional
operational costs associated with booking the group and the
average length of stay of the displaced room nights.

Group Pricing

When it comes to group pricing, assuming you don't already
have an agreed upon rate with the hotel as a company or with a
travel agent, figure out what would be the best rate to offer a
group in order to win its business away from your competitors.

One great way to do this is to first look at the groups you did
"win" in the past and see what rates you offered them in
situations with similar circumstances. For example, let's say in
January of last year you received a group request for a June

booking. You offered a room rate of one hundred Euros per night and won that business. It might be a good idea, then, if you receive another group request for June in January of this year to offer a similar rate.

It's also very important to look at the lead time of the request. In this example, a request received in January for a booking in June has a five-month lead time. However, if you receive the request in May for the June booking—a one-month lead time— then you probably want to offer a different rate.

When doing this exercise, be sure to factor in lead time and season. Make a habit of creating documents with this data, which you can easily locate and reference when quoting rates to future groups.

A similar exercise inverts this process, allowing you to evaluate the groups you lost, rather than won. Determine at what rates you lose most groups for different lead times. I strongly suggest that you implement a system where you can—once a year or, preferably, once a month—evaluate all the lost business to see how you can approach rate setting differently in the future.

Forecasting

Forecasting is where we focus a lot of our attention on the booking pace.

In my previous book, *Revenue Superstar*, I discuss the different ways to approach forecasting. The best way is the action-based forecast. This is where we use pace analytics to identify revenue opportunities and challenges.

So why do we call it *action-based*? It's action-based because we use the current booking pace for a specific period to see if we are in line with where we have to be at this particular point in time to reach our target. Once we recognize that a certain period is behind our target pace, we take a closer look to see what kind of business is underperforming. If your group segments are behind in pace you might have to find replacements in other segments. This is the stage at which you set the commercial action that will drive these new revenue streams. In this example, you might have to find replacement from transient channels such as setting up an online promotion.

Pace

How do you calculate pace? Normally a revenue management system would help you with this, but again, a very simple example will show you how it works.

In this pace case we include 4 parameters:

- Period Target/Budget
- Result Last Year
- On The Books
- On The Books at the Same Point/Period in Time Last Year

Example:

Today is May 1st, and you are making a forecast for June. Here is the data you need to work with:

- **On The Books for June** = 4876 room nights
- **On The Books at the Same Point/Period in time Last Year** = 5054 room nights
- **Period Target/Budget** = 5850 room nights
- **Result Last Year** = 5700 room nights

In this example, we need to sell 150 room nights more than we sold last year to reach our goal. In essence, because our target is higher than the previous year, that means we're already behind our target by 150 room nights.

$$5700 - 5850 = -150$$

At the moment, though, we have also sold 178 fewer room nights compared with what we sold during the same period last year.

$$4876 - 5054 = -178$$

Our current pace, therefore, is −328 room nights.

$$-150 + -178 = -328.$$

This means we are 328 room nights behind where we should be right now to reach our goal, assuming the pace is similar to last year.

In the graph below, we can see how the pace evolved over time. The result last year is obviously static, which would normally make it the target. However, the On The Books figures change every day, giving us the indications and insights we need to set actions.

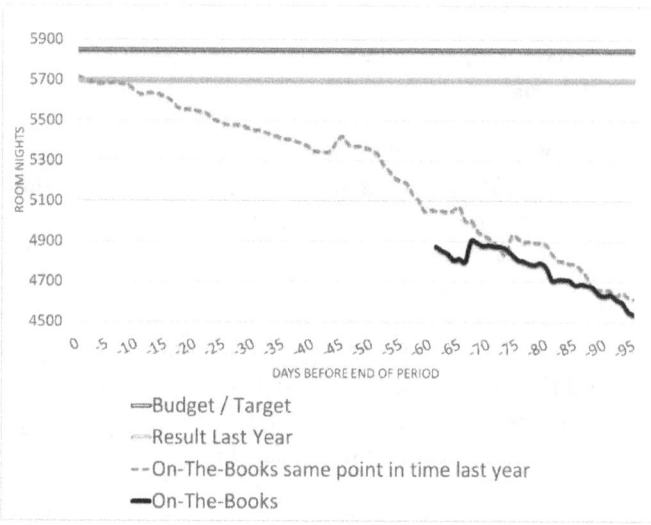

As discussed in the opening chapter on KPIs, this is a highly actionable insight that can be acted upon quickly.

Set actions

Create actions where you see opportunities. Ask yourself: Can I over perform in one segment or rate category to help compensate for loss in another?

Be sure to follow up on previous actions created last month. Are they working: yes or no? If not, you must quickly pivot in another direction.

The actions you set should be included in the new estimations you set for the month.

Campaigns and Promotions

Promotions and advertising are a great way to find incremental business for your hotel. It is important that you figure out what works for your hotel, while continuing to test new ideas.

When considering setting up a campaign for your hotel, ask yourself the following questions:

Why do I need a promotion or campaign?
When should the campaign be valid? (Travel dates and/or booking dates.)
What should the campaign include? What is your offering? (Room types, other rate inclusions.)
Where should it be available? (Which channels, websites, etc.)
Whom should it be available to? (Will you put any restrictions upon the campaign, such as a minimum length of stay? Should it only be available for specific markets?)

Promotions are a great tool to attract extra demand for slow periods, or just to fly beneath the radar of your competitors. However, remember to plan them well in advance using the five Ws above. Do not set up last-minute promotions with poor fences, which will only cannibalize the same demand that you would have booked anyway.

I believe one of the best types of promotions is one in which you package the room with something else. For example, hotel + flight. The smart thing about this combination is that it allows you to offer a compelling rate, which is only visible to somebody who searches for hotel + flight.

Non-pricing campaigns

Non-pricing refers to the strategy of creating a promotion where you do not offer a discount on your public rates. This is a great tactic to use in order to fly below the radar of your competitors during slow periods.

Here are some examples of how to create a promotion without lowering your public rates:

- ✓ Upgrades – offer discounts only on upgraded rooms
- ✓ Packages – only offer a discount if the room is booked as part of a package (ex. flight + hotel)
- ✓ Double member points
- ✓ Added value – offer promotions that include a drink voucher for the hotel bar

Go all in when you create promotions

Do not create a promo, then just sit back and watch what happens. Use all available tools to stimulate as much demand as possible. Depending on which vendors you work with to publish your promos, see if they offer any additional tools that will give your promotions greater visibility. One such example is the Travel Ads tool Expedia offers.

Travel Ads gives you premium placement above the normal list of hotels. You do not pay an extra commission; instead, you pay per click. I have tested this one with a very good return on investment. For example, the last Travel Ad I used, returned twenty-five times the amount of money invested in it.

Expedia's Travel Ads also allow you to write your own headline and teaser text, allowing you to get creative and further separate yourself from the competition.

Part 2: The Revenue Playbook

*"Knowledge without practice is useless.
Practice without knowledge is dangerous."*

— Confucius

Now that we have discussed and provided examples for some numbers, terms, strategies, and promotional ideas, let's bring everything together and put it into practice...

The rest of the book is your personal Revenue Playbook! It is a journal that should be used as a tool to help you manage your daily challenges as a revenue manager.

There are 5 different pages in the journal. I will introduce each page here, then go into more detail before showing you an example of what each page in the journal looks like. In addition to the multiple copies of each journal page provided in this book, you can download PDF versions of these pages at www.revenuesuperstar.com/playbook.

1. The Daily/Weekly Revenue Planner

This is where you plan your day and take notes on important things such as special pricing decisions, competitor movements and market trends.

2. Forecasting

Here's your forecasting companion. Set your pace and the actions you will take. This is a great way to keep track of your actions, see how things evolve over time and plan adjustments for the next time you set your pace and take action.

3. Campaigns & Promotions

These pages are designed to maintain a comprehensive overview of your different campaigns and promotions. They are a good way to remember everything that is active and what worked well in the past.

4. Hotel Reputation overview

Keep track of your online reputation and see how it evolves over time.

5. Braindump

This is your notepad. This can be anything. Plan your budget, set long-term revenue goals or take notes during a revenue meeting.

Daily/Weekly Revenue Planner

These pages are designed for you to use on a daily basis. The reason I like to call it Daily/Weekly is because if your hotel is pretty small or if you aren't located in a major market, then maybe you don't need to do this stuff every day. In such cases, you could use one page per week instead of one per day.

How to use this page:

1. **DAILY 3**
   Record the three most important things you have to do that day (or week). These should normally be tasks where the overall revenue return for the hotel will be very high.
   One example could be to set up a campaign or follow up on actions you set on the last forecast.

2. **PRICING HIGHLIGHTS & LOWLIGHTS**
   Include daily notes from pricing activities and noteworthy decisions like special restrictions or pricing changes. Did you spot any special movements by your competitors today? It is also a good place to write down related things you need to remember for tomorrow or later.

3. **TREND STACKING**
   What specific headlines or hospitality related news jumped out at you the most today?

4. **NOTES**
   This can be anything. Your scratchpad for notes or drawings.

DAY OR WEEK _____

DAILY 3

What are the three most important things I have to do today?

1. _____ ◯
2. _____ ◯
3. _____ ◯

PRICING HIGHLIGHTS & LOWLIGHTS

Daily notes on pricing activities

_____

_____

_____

_____

TREND STACKING

Specific headlines or hospitality related news

_____

_____

_____

MORE NOTES (or drawings ☺)

DAY OR WEEK _____

DAILY 3

What are the three most important things I have to do today?

1. _____ ○

2. _____ ○

3. _____ ○

PRICING HIGHLIGHTS & LOWLIGHTS

Daily notes on pricing activities

_____

_____

_____

_____

TREND STACKING

Specific headlines or hospitality related news

_____

_____

_____

MORE NOTES (or drawings ☺)

DAY OR WEEK _____

DAILY 3
What are the three most important things I have to do today?

1. _____ ◯
2. _____ ◯
3. _____ ◯

PRICING HIGHLIGHTS & LOWLIGHTS
Daily notes on pricing activities

_____

_____

_____

_____

TREND STACKING
Specific headlines or hospitality related news

_____

_____

_____

MORE NOTES (or drawings ☺)

DAY OR WEEK _____

DAILY 3

What are the three most important things I have to do today?

1. _____ ○

2. _____ ○

3. _____ ○

PRICING HIGHLIGHTS & LOWLIGHTS

Daily notes on pricing activities

_____

_____

_____

_____

TREND STACKING

Specific headlines or hospitality related news

_____

_____

_____

MORE NOTES (or drawings ☺)

DAY OR WEEK _____

DAILY 3

What are the three most important things I have to do today?

1. _____ ◯

2. _____ ◯

3. _____ ◯

PRICING HIGHLIGHTS & LOWLIGHTS

Daily notes on pricing activities

_____

_____

_____

_____

TREND STACKING

Specific headlines or hospitality related news

_____

_____

_____

MORE NOTES (or drawings ☺)

DAY OR WEEK _____

DAILY 3

What are the three most important things I have to do today?

1. _____ ○
2. _____ ○
3. _____ ○

PRICING HIGHLIGHTS & LOWLIGHTS

Daily notes on pricing activities

_____

_____

_____

_____

TREND STACKING

Specific headlines or hospitality related news

_____

_____

_____

MORE NOTES (or drawings ☺)

DAY OR WEEK

DAILY 3

What are the three most important things I have to do today?

1. _____ ◯
2. _____ ◯
3. _____ ◯

PRICING HIGHLIGHTS & LOWLIGHTS

Daily notes on pricing activities

_____

_____

_____

_____

TREND STACKING

Specific headlines or hospitality related news

_____

_____

_____

MORE NOTES (or drawings ☺)

DAY OR WEEK _____

DAILY 3

What are the three most important things I have to do today?

1. _____ ○

2. _____ ○

3. _____ ○

PRICING HIGHLIGHTS & LOWLIGHTS

Daily notes on pricing activities

_____

_____

_____

_____

TREND STACKING

Specific headlines or hospitality related news

_____

_____

_____

MORE NOTES (or drawings ☺)

DAY OR WEEK _____

DAILY 3

What are the three most important things I have to do today?

1. _____ ○
2. _____ ○
3. _____ ○

PRICING HIGHLIGHTS & LOWLIGHTS

Daily notes on pricing activities

_____

_____

_____

_____

TREND STACKING

Specific headlines or hospitality related news

_____

_____

_____

_____

MORE NOTES (or drawings ☺)

DAY OR WEEK _____

DAILY 3

What are the three most important things I have to do today?

1. _____ ◯

2. _____ ◯

3. _____ ◯

PRICING HIGHLIGHTS & LOWLIGHTS

Daily notes on pricing activities

_____

_____

_____

_____

TREND STACKING

Specific headlines or hospitality related news

_____

_____

_____

MORE NOTES (or drawings ☺)

DAY OR WEEK

DAILY 3

What are the three most important things I have to do today?

1. _____ ◯

2. _____ ◯

3. _____ ◯

PRICING HIGHLIGHTS & LOWLIGHTS

Daily notes on pricing activities

_____

_____

_____

_____

TREND STACKING

Specific headlines or hospitality related news

_____

_____

_____

MORE NOTES (or drawings ☺)

DAY OR WEEK _____

DAILY 3

What are the three most important things I have to do today?

1. _____ ○
2. _____ ○
3. _____ ○

PRICING HIGHLIGHTS & LOWLIGHTS

Daily notes on pricing activities

_____

_____

_____

_____

TREND STACKING

Specific headlines or hospitality related news

_____

_____

_____

MORE NOTES (or drawings ☺)

DAY OR WEEK

DAILY 3

What are the three most important things I have to do today?

1. _____ ◯

2. _____ ◯

3. _____ ◯

PRICING HIGHLIGHTS & LOWLIGHTS

Daily notes on pricing activities

_____

_____

_____

_____

TREND STACKING

Specific headlines or hospitality related news

_____

_____

_____

MORE NOTES (or drawings ☺)

DAY OR WEEK _____

DAILY 3

What are the three most important things I have to do today?

1. _____ ○
2. _____ ○
3. _____ ○

PRICING HIGHLIGHTS & LOWLIGHTS

Daily notes on pricing activities

_____

_____

_____

_____

TREND STACKING

Specific headlines or hospitality related news

_____

_____

_____

MORE NOTES (or drawings 🙂)

DAY OR WEEK

DAILY 3

What are the three most important things I have to do today?

1. _____ ◯

2. _____ ◯

3. _____ ◯

PRICING HIGHLIGHTS & LOWLIGHTS

Daily notes on pricing activities

_____

_____

_____

_____

TREND STACKING

Specific headlines or hospitality related news

_____

_____

_____

MORE NOTES (or drawings ☺)

DAY OR WEEK _____

DAILY 3

What are the three most important things I have to do today?

1. _____ ◯
2. _____ ◯
3. _____ ◯

PRICING HIGHLIGHTS & LOWLIGHTS

Daily notes on pricing activities

_____

_____

_____

_____

TREND STACKING

Specific headlines or hospitality related news

_____

_____

_____

MORE NOTES (or drawings ☺)

DAY OR WEEK _____

DAILY 3

What are the three most important things I have to do today?

1. _____ ◯
2. _____ ◯
3. _____ ◯

PRICING HIGHLIGHTS & LOWLIGHTS

Daily notes on pricing activities

_____

_____

_____

_____

TREND STACKING

Specific headlines or hospitality related news

_____

_____

_____

MORE NOTES (or drawings ☺)

DAY OR WEEK _____

DAILY 3
What are the three most important things I have to do today?

1. _____ ◯
2. _____ ◯
3. _____ ◯

PRICING HIGHLIGHTS & LOWLIGHTS
Daily notes on pricing activities

_____

_____

_____

_____

TREND STACKING
Specific headlines or hospitality related news

_____

_____

_____

MORE NOTES (or drawings ☺ **)**

DAY OR WEEK

DAILY 3
What are the three most important things I have to do today?

1. _____ ◯

2. _____ ◯

3. _____ ◯

PRICING HIGHLIGHTS & LOWLIGHTS
Daily notes on pricing activities

_____

_____

_____

_____

TREND STACKING
Specific headlines or hospitality related news

_____

_____

_____

MORE NOTES (or drawings ☺)

DAY OR WEEK _____

DAILY 3

What are the three most important things I have to do today?

1. _____ ○

2. _____ ○

3. _____ ○

PRICING HIGHLIGHTS & LOWLIGHTS

Daily notes on pricing activities

_____

_____

_____

_____

TREND STACKING

Specific headlines or hospitality related news

_____

_____

_____

MORE NOTES (or drawings ☺)

DAY OR WEEK

DAILY 3

What are the three most important things I have to do today?

1. _____ ○
2. _____ ○
3. _____ ○

PRICING HIGHLIGHTS & LOWLIGHTS

Daily notes on pricing activities

_____

_____

_____

_____

TREND STACKING

Specific headlines or hospitality related news

_____

_____

_____

MORE NOTES (or drawings ☺)

DAY OR WEEK _____

DAILY 3

What are the three most important things I have to do today?

1. _____ ◯
2. _____ ◯
3. _____ ◯

PRICING HIGHLIGHTS & LOWLIGHTS

Daily notes on pricing activities

_____

_____

_____

_____

TREND STACKING

Specific headlines or hospitality related news

_____

_____

_____

MORE NOTES (or drawings ☺)

DAY OR WEEK

DAILY 3

What are the three most important things I have to do today?

1. _____ ○

2. _____ ○

3. _____ ○

PRICING HIGHLIGHTS & LOWLIGHTS

Daily notes on pricing activities

_____

_____

_____

_____

TREND STACKING

Specific headlines or hospitality related news

_____

_____

_____

MORE NOTES (or drawings ☺)

DAY OR WEEK _____

DAILY 3

What are the three most important things I have to do today?

1. _____ ◯

2. _____ ◯

3. _____ ◯

PRICING HIGHLIGHTS & LOWLIGHTS

Daily notes on pricing activities

_____

_____

_____

_____

TREND STACKING

Specific headlines or hospitality related news

_____

_____

_____

MORE NOTES (or drawings ☺)

DAY OR WEEK _____

DAILY 3

What are the three most important things I have to do today?

1. _____ ○

2. _____ ○

3. _____ ○

PRICING HIGHLIGHTS & LOWLIGHTS

Daily notes on pricing activities

_____

_____

_____

_____

TREND STACKING

Specific headlines or hospitality related news

_____

_____

_____

MORE NOTES (or drawings ☺)

DAY OR WEEK _____

DAILY 3

What are the three most important things I have to do today?

1. _____ ◯
2. _____ ◯
3. _____ ◯

PRICING HIGHLIGHTS & LOWLIGHTS

Daily notes on pricing activities

_____

_____

_____

_____

TREND STACKING

Specific headlines or hospitality related news

_____

_____

_____

MORE NOTES (or drawings ☺)

DAY OR WEEK

DAILY 3

What are the three most important things I have to do today?

1. _____ ○

2. _____ ○

3. _____ ○

PRICING HIGHLIGHTS & LOWLIGHTS

Daily notes on pricing activities

_____

_____

_____

_____

TREND STACKING

Specific headlines or hospitality related news

_____

_____

_____

MORE NOTES (or drawings ☺)

DAY OR WEEK _____

DAILY 3

What are the three most important things I have to do today?

1. _____ ◯

2. _____ ◯

3. _____ ◯

PRICING HIGHLIGHTS & LOWLIGHTS

Daily notes on pricing activities

_____

_____

_____

_____

TREND STACKING

Specific headlines or hospitality related news

_____

_____

_____

MORE NOTES (or drawings ☺)

DAY OR WEEK

DAILY 3

What are the three most important things I have to do today?

1. _____ ○

2. _____ ○

3. _____ ○

PRICING HIGHLIGHTS & LOWLIGHTS

Daily notes on pricing activities

_____

_____

_____

_____

TREND STACKING

Specific headlines or hospitality related news

_____

_____

_____

MORE NOTES (or drawings ☺)

DAY OR WEEK _____

DAILY 3

What are the three most important things I have to do today?

1. _____ ◯

2. _____ ◯

3. _____ ◯

PRICING HIGHLIGHTS & LOWLIGHTS

Daily notes on pricing activities

_____

_____

_____

_____

TREND STACKING

Specific headlines or hospitality related news

_____

_____

_____

MORE NOTES (or drawings ☺)

DAY OR WEEK _____

DAILY 3

What are the three most important things I have to do today?

1. _____ ○

2. _____ ○

3. _____ ○

PRICING HIGHLIGHTS & LOWLIGHTS

Daily notes on pricing activities

_____

_____

_____

_____

TREND STACKING

Specific headlines or hospitality related news

_____

_____

_____

MORE NOTES (or drawings ☺)

DAY OR WEEK _____

DAILY 3

What are the three most important things I have to do today?

1. _____ ◯
2. _____ ◯
3. _____ ◯

PRICING HIGHLIGHTS & LOWLIGHTS

Daily notes on pricing activities

_____

_____

_____

_____

TREND STACKING

Specific headlines or hospitality related news

_____

_____

_____

MORE NOTES (or drawings ☺)

DAY OR WEEK _____

DAILY 3

What are the three most important things I have to do today?

1. _____ ○

2. _____ ○

3. _____ ○

PRICING HIGHLIGHTS & LOWLIGHTS

Daily notes on pricing activities

_____

_____

_____

_____

TREND STACKING

Specific headlines or hospitality related news

_____

_____

_____

MORE NOTES (or drawings ☺)

DAY OR WEEK _____

DAILY 3

What are the three most important things I have to do today?

1. _____ ◯

2. _____ ◯

3. _____ ◯

PRICING HIGHLIGHTS & LOWLIGHTS

Daily notes on pricing activities

_____

_____

_____

_____

TREND STACKING

Specific headlines or hospitality related news

_____

_____

_____

MORE NOTES (or drawings ☺)

DAY OR WEEK

DAILY 3

What are the three most important things I have to do today?

1. _____ ○
2. _____ ○
3. _____ ○

PRICING HIGHLIGHTS & LOWLIGHTS

Daily notes on pricing activities

_____

_____

_____

_____

TREND STACKING

Specific headlines or hospitality related news

_____

_____

_____

MORE NOTES (or drawings ☺)

DAY OR WEEK _____

DAILY 3

What are the three most important things I have to do today?

1. _____ ○
2. _____ ○
3. _____ ○

PRICING HIGHLIGHTS & LOWLIGHTS

Daily notes on pricing activities

_____

_____

_____

_____

TREND STACKING

Specific headlines or hospitality related news

_____

_____

_____

MORE NOTES (or drawings ☺)

DAY OR WEEK   _____

DAILY 3

What are the three most important things I have to do today?

1. _____ ◯

2. _____ ◯

3. _____ ◯

PRICING HIGHLIGHTS & LOWLIGHTS

Daily notes on pricing activities

_____

_____

_____

_____

TREND STACKING

Specific headlines or hospitality related news

_____

_____

_____

MORE NOTES (or drawings ☺)

DAY OR WEEK

DAILY 3

What are the three most important things I have to do today?

1. _____ ◯
2. _____ ◯
3. _____ ◯

PRICING HIGHLIGHTS & LOWLIGHTS

Daily notes on pricing activities

_____

_____

_____

_____

TREND STACKING

Specific headlines or hospitality related news

_____

_____

_____

MORE NOTES (or drawings ☺)

DAY OR WEEK

DAILY 3

What are the three most important things I have to do today?

1. _____ ○

2. _____ ○

3. _____ ○

PRICING HIGHLIGHTS & LOWLIGHTS

Daily notes on pricing activities

_____

_____

_____

_____

TREND STACKING

Specific headlines or hospitality related news

_____

_____

_____

MORE NOTES (or drawings ☺)

DAY OR WEEK _____

DAILY 3

What are the three most important things I have to do today?

1. _____ ◯

2. _____ ◯

3. _____ ◯

PRICING HIGHLIGHTS & LOWLIGHTS

Daily notes on pricing activities

_____

_____

_____

_____

TREND STACKING

Specific headlines or hospitality related news

_____

_____

_____

MORE NOTES (or drawings ☺)

DAY OR WEEK

DAILY 3

What are the three most important things I have to do today?

1. _____ ○

2. _____ ○

3. _____ ○

PRICING HIGHLIGHTS & LOWLIGHTS

Daily notes on pricing activities

_____

_____

_____

_____

TREND STACKING

Specific headlines or hospitality related news

_____

_____

_____

MORE NOTES (or drawings ☺)

DAY OR WEEK

DAILY 3

What are the three most important things I have to do today?

1. _____ ◯
2. _____ ◯
3. _____ ◯

PRICING HIGHLIGHTS & LOWLIGHTS

Daily notes on pricing activities

_____

_____

_____

_____

TREND STACKING

Specific headlines or hospitality related news

_____

_____

_____

MORE NOTES (or drawings ☺)

DAY OR WEEK

DAILY 3

What are the three most important things I have to do today?

1. _____ ◯

2. _____ ◯

3. _____ ◯

PRICING HIGHLIGHTS & LOWLIGHTS

Daily notes on pricing activities

_____

_____

_____

_____

TREND STACKING

Specific headlines or hospitality related news

_____

_____

_____

MORE NOTES (or drawings ☺)

DAY OR WEEK _____

DAILY 3

What are the three most important things I have to do today?

1. _____ ◯

2. _____ ◯

3. _____ ◯

PRICING HIGHLIGHTS & LOWLIGHTS

Daily notes on pricing activities

_____

_____

_____

_____

TREND STACKING

Specific headlines or hospitality related news

_____

_____

_____

MORE NOTES (or drawings ☺)

DAY OR WEEK _____

DAILY 3

What are the three most important things I have to do today?

1. _____ ◯

2. _____ ◯

3. _____ ◯

PRICING HIGHLIGHTS & LOWLIGHTS

Daily notes on pricing activities

_____

_____

_____

_____

TREND STACKING

Specific headlines or hospitality related news

_____

_____

_____

MORE NOTES (or drawings ☺)

DAY OR WEEK _____

DAILY 3

What are the three most important things I have to do today?

1. _____ ◯
2. _____ ◯
3. _____ ◯

PRICING HIGHLIGHTS & LOWLIGHTS

Daily notes on pricing activities

_____
_____
_____
_____

TREND STACKING

Specific headlines or hospitality related news

_____
_____
_____

MORE NOTES (or drawings ☺)

DAY OR WEEK _____

DAILY 3

What are the three most important things I have to do today?

1. _____ ◯
2. _____ ◯
3. _____ ◯

PRICING HIGHLIGHTS & LOWLIGHTS

Daily notes on pricing activities

_____

_____

_____

_____

TREND STACKING

Specific headlines or hospitality related news

_____

_____

_____

MORE NOTES (or drawings ☺)

DAY OR WEEK _____

DAILY 3

What are the three most important things I have to do today?

1. _____ ○

2. _____ ○

3. _____ ○

PRICING HIGHLIGHTS & LOWLIGHTS

Daily notes on pricing activities

_____

_____

_____

_____

TREND STACKING

Specific headlines or hospitality related news

_____

_____

_____

MORE NOTES (or drawings ☺)

DAY OR WEEK

DAILY 3

What are the three most important things I have to do today?

1. _____ ◯

2. _____ ◯

3. _____ ◯

PRICING HIGHLIGHTS & LOWLIGHTS

Daily notes on pricing activities

_____

_____

_____

_____

TREND STACKING

Specific headlines or hospitality related news

_____

_____

_____

MORE NOTES (or drawings ☺)

DAY OR WEEK _____

DAILY 3

What are the three most important things I have to do today?

1. _____ ◯

2. _____ ◯

3. _____ ◯

PRICING HIGHLIGHTS & LOWLIGHTS

Daily notes on pricing activities

_____

_____

_____

_____

TREND STACKING

Specific headlines or hospitality related news

_____

_____

_____

MORE NOTES (or drawings ☺)

DAY OR WEEK

DAILY 3

What are the three most important things I have to do today?

1. _____ ○

2. _____ ○

3. _____ ○

PRICING HIGHLIGHTS & LOWLIGHTS

Daily notes on pricing activities

_____

_____

_____

_____

TREND STACKING

Specific headlines or hospitality related news

_____

_____

_____

MORE NOTES (or drawings ☺)

DAY OR WEEK

DAILY 3
What are the three most important things I have to do today?

1. _____ ◯
2. _____ ◯
3. _____ ◯

PRICING HIGHLIGHTS & LOWLIGHTS
Daily notes on pricing activities

_____

_____

_____

_____

TREND STACKING
Specific headlines or hospitality related news

_____

_____

_____

MORE NOTES (or drawings ☺)

DAY OR WEEK _____

DAILY 3

What are the three most important things I have to do today?

1. _____ ○

2. _____ ○

3. _____ ○

PRICING HIGHLIGHTS & LOWLIGHTS

Daily notes on pricing activities

_____

_____

_____

_____

TREND STACKING

Specific headlines or hospitality related news

_____

_____

_____

MORE NOTES (or drawings ☺)

DAY OR WEEK _____

DAILY 3

What are the three most important things I have to do today?

1. _____ ○

2. _____ ○

3. _____ ○

PRICING HIGHLIGHTS & LOWLIGHTS

Daily notes on pricing activities

_____

_____

_____

_____

TREND STACKING

Specific headlines or hospitality related news

_____

_____

_____

MORE NOTES (or drawings ☺)

DAY OR WEEK _____

DAILY 3

What are the three most important things I have to do today?

1. _____ ◯

2. _____ ◯

3. _____ ◯

PRICING HIGHLIGHTS & LOWLIGHTS

Daily notes on pricing activities

_____

_____

_____

_____

TREND STACKING

Specific headlines or hospitality related news

_____

_____

_____

MORE NOTES (or drawings ☺)

DAY OR WEEK _____

DAILY 3

What are the three most important things I have to do today?

1. _____ ◯

2. _____ ◯

3. _____ ◯

PRICING HIGHLIGHTS & LOWLIGHTS

Daily notes on pricing activities

_____

_____

_____

_____

TREND STACKING

Specific headlines or hospitality related news

_____

_____

_____

MORE NOTES (or drawings ☺)

DAY OR WEEK _____

DAILY 3

What are the three most important things I have to do today?

1. _____ ◯

2. _____ ◯

3. _____ ◯

PRICING HIGHLIGHTS & LOWLIGHTS

Daily notes on pricing activities

_____

_____

_____

_____

TREND STACKING

Specific headlines or hospitality related news

_____

_____

_____

MORE NOTES (or drawings ☺)

DAY OR WEEK _____

DAILY 3

What are the three most important things I have to do today?

1. _____ ◯

2. _____ ◯

3. _____ ◯

PRICING HIGHLIGHTS & LOWLIGHTS

Daily notes on pricing activities

_____

_____

_____

_____

TREND STACKING

Specific headlines or hospitality related news

_____

_____

_____

MORE NOTES (or drawings ☺)

DAY OR WEEK

DAILY 3
What are the three most important things I have to do today?

1. _____ ○

2. _____ ○

3. _____ ○

PRICING HIGHLIGHTS & LOWLIGHTS
Daily notes on pricing activities

_____

_____

_____

_____

TREND STACKING
Specific headlines or hospitality related news

_____

_____

_____

MORE NOTES (or drawings ☺)

DAY OR WEEK _____

DAILY 3

What are the three most important things I have to do today?

1. _____ ◯

2. _____ ◯

3. _____ ◯

PRICING HIGHLIGHTS & LOWLIGHTS

Daily notes on pricing activities

_____

_____

_____

_____

TREND STACKING

Specific headlines or hospitality related news

_____

_____

_____

MORE NOTES (or drawings ☺)

DAY OR WEEK

DAILY 3
What are the three most important things I have to do today?

1. _____ ◯

2. _____ ◯

3. _____ ◯

PRICING HIGHLIGHTS & LOWLIGHTS
Daily notes on pricing activities

_____

_____

_____

_____

TREND STACKING
Specific headlines or hospitality related news

_____

_____

_____

MORE NOTES (or drawings ☺)

DAY OR WEEK _____

DAILY 3

What are the three most important things I have to do today?

1. _____ ○
2. _____ ○
3. _____ ○

PRICING HIGHLIGHTS & LOWLIGHTS

Daily notes on pricing activities

_____

_____

_____

_____

TREND STACKING

Specific headlines or hospitality related news

_____

_____

_____

MORE NOTES (or drawings ☺)

DAY OR WEEK

DAILY 3

What are the three most important things I have to do today?

1. _____ ◯

2. _____ ◯

3. _____ ◯

PRICING HIGHLIGHTS & LOWLIGHTS

Daily notes on pricing activities

_____

_____

_____

_____

TREND STACKING

Specific headlines or hospitality related news

_____

_____

_____

MORE NOTES (or drawings ☺)

DAY OR WEEK _____

DAILY 3

What are the three most important things I have to do today?

1. _____ ○

2. _____ ○

3. _____ ○

PRICING HIGHLIGHTS & LOWLIGHTS

Daily notes on pricing activities

_____

_____

_____

_____

TREND STACKING

Specific headlines or hospitality related news

_____

_____

_____

MORE NOTES (or drawings ☺)

DAY OR WEEK

DAILY 3

What are the three most important things I have to do today?

1. _____ ◯
2. _____ ◯
3. _____ ◯

PRICING HIGHLIGHTS & LOWLIGHTS

Daily notes on pricing activities

_____

_____

_____

_____

TREND STACKING

Specific headlines or hospitality related news

_____

_____

_____

MORE NOTES (or drawings ☺)

DAY OR WEEK _____

DAILY 3

What are the three most important things I have to do today?

1. _____ ○

2. _____ ○

3. _____ ○

PRICING HIGHLIGHTS & LOWLIGHTS

Daily notes on pricing activities

_____

_____

_____

_____

TREND STACKING

Specific headlines or hospitality related news

_____

_____

_____

MORE NOTES (or drawings ☺)

DAY OR WEEK

DAILY 3
What are the three most important things I have to do today?

1. _____ ◯
2. _____ ◯
3. _____ ◯

PRICING HIGHLIGHTS & LOWLIGHTS
Daily notes on pricing activities

_____

_____

_____

_____

TREND STACKING
Specific headlines or hospitality related news

_____

_____

_____

MORE NOTES (or drawings ☺)

DAY OR WEEK _____

DAILY 3

What are the three most important things I have to do today?

1. _____ ○

2. _____ ○

3. _____ ○

PRICING HIGHLIGHTS & LOWLIGHTS

Daily notes on pricing activities

_____

_____

_____

_____

TREND STACKING

Specific headlines or hospitality related news

_____

_____

_____

MORE NOTES (or drawings ☺)

DAY OR WEEK

DAILY 3

What are the three most important things I have to do today?

1. _____ ○

2. _____ ○

3. _____ ○

PRICING HIGHLIGHTS & LOWLIGHTS

Daily notes on pricing activities

_____

_____

_____

_____

TREND STACKING

Specific headlines or hospitality related news

_____

_____

_____

MORE NOTES (or drawings ☺)

DAY OR WEEK _____

DAILY 3

What are the three most important things I have to do today?

1. _____ ◯

2. _____ ◯

3. _____ ◯

PRICING HIGHLIGHTS & LOWLIGHTS

Daily notes on pricing activities

_____

_____

_____

_____

TREND STACKING

Specific headlines or hospitality related news

_____

_____

_____

MORE NOTES (or drawings ☺)

DAY OR WEEK _____

DAILY 3
What are the three most important things I have to do today?

1. _____ ◯
2. _____ ◯
3. _____ ◯

PRICING HIGHLIGHTS & LOWLIGHTS
Daily notes on pricing activities

_____

_____

_____

_____

TREND STACKING
Specific headlines or hospitality related news

_____

_____

_____

MORE NOTES (or drawings ☺)

DAY OR WEEK _____

DAILY 3

What are the three most important things I have to do today?

1. _____ ◯
2. _____ ◯
3. _____ ◯

PRICING HIGHLIGHTS & LOWLIGHTS

Daily notes on pricing activities

_____

_____

_____

_____

TREND STACKING

Specific headlines or hospitality related news

_____

_____

_____

MORE NOTES (or drawings ☺)

DAY OR WEEK _____

DAILY 3

What are the three most important things I have to do today?

1. _____ ◯

2. _____ ◯

3. _____ ◯

PRICING HIGHLIGHTS & LOWLIGHTS

Daily notes on pricing activities

_____

_____

_____

_____

TREND STACKING

Specific headlines or hospitality related news

_____

_____

_____

MORE NOTES (or drawings ☺)

DAY OR WEEK _____

DAILY 3

What are the three most important things I have to do today?

1. _____ ◯

2. _____ ◯

3. _____ ◯

PRICING HIGHLIGHTS & LOWLIGHTS

Daily notes on pricing activities

_____

_____

_____

_____

TREND STACKING

Specific headlines or hospitality related news

_____

_____

_____

MORE NOTES (or drawings ☺)

DAY OR WEEK

DAILY 3

What are the three most important things I have to do today?

1. _____ ○

2. _____ ○

3. _____ ○

PRICING HIGHLIGHTS & LOWLIGHTS

Daily notes on pricing activities

_____

_____

_____

_____

TREND STACKING

Specific headlines or hospitality related news

_____

_____

_____

MORE NOTES (or drawings ☺)

DAY OR WEEK _____

DAILY 3
What are the three most important things I have to do today?

1. _____ ◯
2. _____ ◯
3. _____ ◯

PRICING HIGHLIGHTS & LOWLIGHTS
Daily notes on pricing activities

_____

_____

_____

_____

TREND STACKING
Specific headlines or hospitality related news

_____

_____

_____

MORE NOTES (or drawings ☺)

DAY OR WEEK _____

DAILY 3

What are the three most important things I have to do today?

1. _____ ○

2. _____ ○

3. _____ ○

PRICING HIGHLIGHTS & LOWLIGHTS

Daily notes on pricing activities

_____

_____

_____

_____

TREND STACKING

Specific headlines or hospitality related news

_____

_____

_____

MORE NOTES (or drawings ☺)

DAY OR WEEK _____

DAILY 3
What are the three most important things I have to do today?

1. _____ ○
2. _____ ○
3. _____ ○

PRICING HIGHLIGHTS & LOWLIGHTS
Daily notes on pricing activities

_____

_____

_____

_____

TREND STACKING
Specific headlines or hospitality related news

_____

_____

_____

MORE NOTES (or drawings ☺)

DAY OR WEEK

DAILY 3
What are the three most important things I have to do today?

1. _____ ◯
2. _____ ◯
3. _____ ◯

PRICING HIGHLIGHTS & LOWLIGHTS
Daily notes on pricing activities

_____

_____

_____

_____

TREND STACKING
Specific headlines or hospitality related news

_____

_____

_____

MORE NOTES (or drawings ☺)

DAY OR WEEK _____

DAILY 3

What are the three most important things I have to do today?

1. _____ ○

2. _____ ○

3. _____ ○

PRICING HIGHLIGHTS & LOWLIGHTS

Daily notes on pricing activities

_____

_____

_____

_____

TREND STACKING

Specific headlines or hospitality related news

_____

_____

_____

MORE NOTES (or drawings ☺)

DAY OR WEEK

DAILY 3

What are the three most important things I have to do today?

1. _____ ◯
2. _____ ◯
3. _____ ◯

PRICING HIGHLIGHTS & LOWLIGHTS

Daily notes on pricing activities

_____

_____

_____

_____

TREND STACKING

Specific headlines or hospitality related news

_____

_____

_____

MORE NOTES (or drawings ☺)

DAY OR WEEK _____

DAILY 3

What are the three most important things I have to do today?

1. _____ ◯

2. _____ ◯

3. _____ ◯

PRICING HIGHLIGHTS & LOWLIGHTS

Daily notes on pricing activities

_____

_____

_____

_____

TREND STACKING

Specific headlines or hospitality related news

_____

_____

_____

MORE NOTES (or drawings ☺)

DAY OR WEEK

DAILY 3

What are the three most important things I have to do today?

1. _____ ◯
2. _____ ◯
3. _____ ◯

PRICING HIGHLIGHTS & LOWLIGHTS

Daily notes on pricing activities

_____

_____

_____

_____

TREND STACKING

Specific headlines or hospitality related news

_____

_____

_____

MORE NOTES (or drawings ☺)

DAY OR WEEK _____

DAILY 3

What are the three most important things I have to do today?

1. _____ ◯
2. _____ ◯
3. _____ ◯

PRICING HIGHLIGHTS & LOWLIGHTS

Daily notes on pricing activities

_____

_____

_____

_____

TREND STACKING

Specific headlines or hospitality related news

_____

_____

_____

MORE NOTES (or drawings ☺)

DAY OR WEEK _____

DAILY 3

What are the three most important things I have to do today?

1. _____ ◯
2. _____ ◯
3. _____ ◯

PRICING HIGHLIGHTS & LOWLIGHTS

Daily notes on pricing activities

_____

_____

_____

_____

TREND STACKING

Specific headlines or hospitality related news

_____

_____

_____

MORE NOTES (or drawings ☺)

DAY OR WEEK _____

DAILY 3

What are the three most important things I have to do today?

1. _____ ◯
2. _____ ◯
3. _____ ◯

PRICING HIGHLIGHTS & LOWLIGHTS

Daily notes on pricing activities

_____

_____

_____

_____

TREND STACKING

Specific headlines or hospitality related news

_____

_____

_____

MORE NOTES (or drawings ☺ **)**

DAY OR WEEK

DAILY 3
What are the three most important things I have to do today?

1. _____ ◯
2. _____ ◯
3. _____ ◯

PRICING HIGHLIGHTS & LOWLIGHTS
Daily notes on pricing activities

_____
_____
_____
_____

TREND STACKING
Specific headlines or hospitality related news

_____
_____
_____

MORE NOTES (or drawings ☺)

DAY OR WEEK

DAILY 3

What are the three most important things I have to do today?

1. _____ ○

2. _____ ○

3. _____ ○

PRICING HIGHLIGHTS & LOWLIGHTS

Daily notes on pricing activities

_____

_____

_____

_____

TREND STACKING

Specific headlines or hospitality related news

_____

_____

_____

MORE NOTES (or drawings ☺)

DAY OR WEEK _____

DAILY 3

What are the three most important things I have to do today?

1. _____ ○
2. _____ ○
3. _____ ○

PRICING HIGHLIGHTS & LOWLIGHTS

Daily notes on pricing activities

_____

_____

_____

_____

TREND STACKING

Specific headlines or hospitality related news

_____

_____

_____

MORE NOTES (or drawings ☺)

DAY OR WEEK _____

DAILY 3

What are the three most important things I have to do today?

1. _____ ◯

2. _____ ◯

3. _____ ◯

PRICING HIGHLIGHTS & LOWLIGHTS

Daily notes on pricing activities

_____

_____

_____

_____

TREND STACKING

Specific headlines or hospitality related news

_____

_____

_____

MORE NOTES (or drawings ☺)

DAY OR WEEK

DAILY 3

What are the three most important things I have to do today?

1. _____ ◯

2. _____ ◯

3. _____ ◯

PRICING HIGHLIGHTS & LOWLIGHTS

Daily notes on pricing activities

_____

_____

_____

_____

TREND STACKING

Specific headlines or hospitality related news

_____

_____

_____

MORE NOTES (or drawings ☺)

DAY OR WEEK _____

DAILY 3

What are the three most important things I have to do today?

1. _____ ○

2. _____ ○

3. _____ ○

PRICING HIGHLIGHTS & LOWLIGHTS

Daily notes on pricing activities

_____

_____

_____

_____

TREND STACKING

Specific headlines or hospitality related news

_____

_____

_____

MORE NOTES (or drawings ☺)

DAY OR WEEK

DAILY 3

What are the three most important things I have to do today?

1. _____ ○

2. _____ ○

3. _____ ○

PRICING HIGHLIGHTS & LOWLIGHTS

Daily notes on pricing activities

_____

_____

_____

_____

TREND STACKING

Specific headlines or hospitality related news

_____

_____

_____

MORE NOTES (or drawings ☺)

DAY OR WEEK _____

DAILY 3

What are the three most important things I have to do today?

1. _____ ◯

2. _____ ◯

3. _____ ◯

PRICING HIGHLIGHTS & LOWLIGHTS

Daily notes on pricing activities

_____

_____

_____

_____

TREND STACKING

Specific headlines or hospitality related news

_____

_____

_____

MORE NOTES (or drawings ☺)

Forecasting Page

This sheet will help you to keep your forecasts organized. For example, if you create a new periodic forecast once a month, this will provide a great way to highlight your current pace and set actions accordingly. Highlight whether a specific segment is underperforming or overperforming.

This will make it very easy for you to go back once a month to check the status of your previous forecasts and to follow up on your actions and make adjustments as necessary.

You can read more about Pace on page 12 and Forecasting on page 20.

FORECASTING

DATE: _____

PERIOD: _____

PACE:
-30%	-20%	-10%	0%	+10%	+20%	+30%
○	○	○	○	○	○	○

ACTIONS:

PERIOD: _____

PACE:
-30%	-20%	-10%	0%	+10%	+20%	+30%
○	○	○	○	○	○	○

ACTIONS:

PERIOD: _____

PACE:
-30%	-20%	-10%	0%	+10%	+20%	+30%
○	○	○	○	○	○	○

ACTIONS:

FORECASTING

PERIOD: _____

PACE:

-30%	-20%	-10%	0%	+10%	+20%	+30%
○	○	○	○	○	○	○

ACTIONS:

PERIOD: _____

PACE:

-30%	-20%	-10%	0%	+10%	+20%	+30%
○	○	○	○	○	○	○

ACTIONS:

PERIOD: _____

PACE:

-30%	-20%	-10%	0%	+10%	+20%	+30%
○	○	○	○	○	○	○

ACTIONS:

FORECASTING

DATE: _____

PERIOD: _____

PACE:	-30%	-20%	-10%	0%	+10%	+20%	+30%
	○	○	○	○	○	○	○

ACTIONS:

PERIOD: _____

PACE:	-30%	-20%	-10%	0%	+10%	+20%	+30%
	○	○	○	○	○	○	○

ACTIONS:

PERIOD: _____

PACE:	-30%	-20%	-10%	0%	+10%	+20%	+30%
	○	○	○	○	○	○	○

ACTIONS:

FORECASTING

DATE: _____

PERIOD: _____

PACE:
| -30% | -20% | -10% | 0% | +10% | +20% | +30% |
| ○ | ○ | ○ | ○ | ○ | ○ | ○ |

ACTIONS:

PERIOD: _____

PACE:
| -30% | -20% | -10% | 0% | +10% | +20% | +30% |
| ○ | ○ | ○ | ○ | ○ | ○ | ○ |

ACTIONS:

PERIOD: _____

PACE:
| -30% | -20% | -10% | 0% | +10% | +20% | +30% |
| ○ | ○ | ○ | ○ | ○ | ○ | ○ |

ACTIONS:

FORECASTING

DATE: _____

PERIOD: _____

PACE:
-30%	-20%	-10%	0%	+10%	+20%	+30%
◯	◯	◯	◯	◯	◯	◯

ACTIONS:

PERIOD: _____

PACE:
-30%	-20%	-10%	0%	+10%	+20%	+30%
◯	◯	◯	◯	◯	◯	◯

ACTIONS:

PERIOD: _____

PACE:
-30%	-20%	-10%	0%	+10%	+20%	+30%
◯	◯	◯	◯	◯	◯	◯

ACTIONS:

FORECASTING

DATE: _____

PERIOD: _____

PACE:

-30%	-20%	-10%	0%	+10%	+20%	+30%
◯	◯	◯	◯	◯	◯	◯

ACTIONS:

PERIOD: _____

PACE:

-30%	-20%	-10%	0%	+10%	+20%	+30%
◯	◯	◯	◯	◯	◯	◯

ACTIONS:

PERIOD: _____

PACE:

-30%	-20%	-10%	0%	+10%	+20%	+30%
◯	◯	◯	◯	◯	◯	◯

ACTIONS:

FORECASTING

DATE: _____

PERIOD: _____

PACE:

-30%	-20%	-10%	0%	+10%	+20%	+30%
◯	◯	◯	◯	◯	◯	◯

ACTIONS:

PERIOD: _____

PACE:

-30%	-20%	-10%	0%	+10%	+20%	+30%
◯	◯	◯	◯	◯	◯	◯

ACTIONS:

PERIOD: _____

PACE:

-30%	-20%	-10%	0%	+10%	+20%	+30%
◯	◯	◯	◯	◯	◯	◯

ACTIONS:

FORECASTING

DATE: _____

PERIOD: _____

PACE:
-30%	-20%	-10%	0%	+10%	+20%	+30%
◯	◯	◯	◯	◯	◯	◯

ACTIONS:

PERIOD: _____

PACE:
-30%	-20%	-10%	0%	+10%	+20%	+30%
◯	◯	◯	◯	◯	◯	◯

ACTIONS:

PERIOD: _____

PACE:
-30%	-20%	-10%	0%	+10%	+20%	+30%
◯	◯	◯	◯	◯	◯	◯

ACTIONS:

FORECASTING

DATE: _____

PERIOD: _____

PACE:
-30%	-20%	-10%	0%	+10%	+20%	+30%
◯	◯	◯	◯	◯	◯	◯

ACTIONS:

PERIOD: _____

PACE:
-30%	-20%	-10%	0%	+10%	+20%	+30%
◯	◯	◯	◯	◯	◯	◯

ACTIONS:

PERIOD: _____

PACE:
-30%	-20%	-10%	0%	+10%	+20%	+30%
◯	◯	◯	◯	◯	◯	◯

ACTIONS:

FORECASTING

DATE: _____

PERIOD: _____

PACE:
-30%	-20%	-10%	0%	+10%	+20%	+30%
◯	◯	◯	◯	◯	◯	◯

ACTIONS:

PERIOD: _____

PACE:
-30%	-20%	-10%	0%	+10%	+20%	+30%
◯	◯	◯	◯	◯	◯	◯

ACTIONS:

PERIOD: _____

PACE:
-30%	-20%	-10%	0%	+10%	+20%	+30%
◯	◯	◯	◯	◯	◯	◯

ACTIONS:

FORECASTING

DATE: _____

PERIOD: _____

PACE:
-30%	-20%	-10%	0%	+10%	+20%	+30%
◯	◯	◯	◯	◯	◯	◯

ACTIONS:

PERIOD: _____

PACE:
-30%	-20%	-10%	0%	+10%	+20%	+30%
◯	◯	◯	◯	◯	◯	◯

ACTIONS:

PERIOD: _____

PACE:
-30%	-20%	-10%	0%	+10%	+20%	+30%
◯	◯	◯	◯	◯	◯	◯

ACTIONS:

FORECASTING

DATE: _____

PERIOD: _____

PACE:
-30%	-20%	-10%	0%	+10%	+20%	+30%
◯	◯	◯	◯	◯	◯	◯

ACTIONS:

PERIOD: _____

PACE:
-30%	-20%	-10%	0%	+10%	+20%	+30%
◯	◯	◯	◯	◯	◯	◯

ACTIONS:

PERIOD: _____

PACE:
-30%	-20%	-10%	0%	+10%	+20%	+30%
◯	◯	◯	◯	◯	◯	◯

ACTIONS:

FORECASTING

DATE: _____

PERIOD: _____

PACE:

| -30% | -20% | -10% | 0% | +10% | +20% | +30% |
| ○ | ○ | ○ | ○ | ○ | ○ | ○ |

ACTIONS:

PERIOD: _____

PACE:

| -30% | -20% | -10% | 0% | +10% | +20% | +30% |
| ○ | ○ | ○ | ○ | ○ | ○ | ○ |

ACTIONS:

PERIOD: _____

PACE:

| -30% | -20% | -10% | 0% | +10% | +20% | +30% |
| ○ | ○ | ○ | ○ | ○ | ○ | ○ |

ACTIONS:

FORECASTING

DATE: _____

PERIOD: _____

PACE:
-30%	-20%	-10%	0%	+10%	+20%	+30%
○	○	○	○	○	○	○

ACTIONS:

PERIOD: _____

PACE:
-30%	-20%	-10%	0%	+10%	+20%	+30%
○	○	○	○	○	○	○

ACTIONS:

PERIOD: _____

PACE:
-30%	-20%	-10%	0%	+10%	+20%	+30%
○	○	○	○	○	○	○

ACTIONS:

FORECASTING

DATE: _____

PERIOD: _____

PACE: -30%   -20%   -10%   0%   +10%   +20%   +30%
         ◯   ◯   ◯   ◯   ◯   ◯   ◯

ACTIONS:

PERIOD: _____

PACE: -30%   -20%   -10%   0%   +10%   +20%   +30%
         ◯   ◯   ◯   ◯   ◯   ◯   ◯

ACTIONS:

PERIOD: _____

PACE: -30%   -20%   -10%   0%   +10%   +20%   +30%
         ◯   ◯   ◯   ◯   ◯   ◯   ◯

ACTIONS:

FORECASTING

DATE: _____

PERIOD: _____

PACE:

-30%	-20%	-10%	0%	+10%	+20%	+30%
◯	◯	◯	◯	◯	◯	◯

ACTIONS:

PERIOD: _____

PACE:

-30%	-20%	-10%	0%	+10%	+20%	+30%
◯	◯	◯	◯	◯	◯	◯

ACTIONS:

PERIOD: _____

PACE:

-30%	-20%	-10%	0%	+10%	+20%	+30%
◯	◯	◯	◯	◯	◯	◯

ACTIONS:

FORECASTING

DATE: _____

PERIOD: _____

PACE:

-30%	-20%	-10%	0%	+10%	+20%	+30%
◯	◯	◯	◯	◯	◯	◯

ACTIONS:

PERIOD: _____

PACE:

-30%	-20%	-10%	0%	+10%	+20%	+30%
◯	◯	◯	◯	◯	◯	◯

ACTIONS:

PERIOD: _____

PACE:

-30%	-20%	-10%	0%	+10%	+20%	+30%
◯	◯	◯	◯	◯	◯	◯

ACTIONS:

FORECASTING

DATE: _____

PERIOD: _____

PACE:
-30%	-20%	-10%	0%	+10%	+20%	+30%
◯	◯	◯	◯	◯	◯	◯

ACTIONS:

PERIOD: _____

PACE:
-30%	-20%	-10%	0%	+10%	+20%	+30%
◯	◯	◯	◯	◯	◯	◯

ACTIONS:

PERIOD: _____

PACE:
-30%	-20%	-10%	0%	+10%	+20%	+30%
◯	◯	◯	◯	◯	◯	◯

ACTIONS:

FORECASTING

DATE: _____

PERIOD: _____

PACE: -30% -20% -10% 0% +10% +20% +30%
        ◯   ◯   ◯   ◯   ◯   ◯   ◯

ACTIONS:

PERIOD: _____

PACE: -30% -20% -10% 0% +10% +20% +30%
        ◯   ◯   ◯   ◯   ◯   ◯   ◯

ACTIONS:

PERIOD: _____

PACE: -30% -20% -10% 0% +10% +20% +30%
        ◯   ◯   ◯   ◯   ◯   ◯   ◯

ACTIONS:

FORECASTING

DATE: _____

PERIOD: _____

PACE:

-30%	-20%	-10%	0%	+10%	+20%	+30%
○	○	○	○	○	○	○

ACTIONS:

PERIOD: _____

PACE:

-30%	-20%	-10%	0%	+10%	+20%	+30%
○	○	○	○	○	○	○

ACTIONS:

PERIOD: _____

PACE:

-30%	-20%	-10%	0%	+10%	+20%	+30%
○	○	○	○	○	○	○

ACTIONS:

Campaigns & Promotions Page

On this sheet you can keep an overview of your ongoing campaigns and promotions.

Write down a campaign's details such as booking period and type of promotion. Once the campaign is over you can enter the result.

Maintaining a comprehensive overview of all of your Campaigns and Promotions will help you to remember which ones were successful and which were not. Knowing which ones worked will allow you to easily go back and copy the successful ones, as well as to come up with creative methods of improving upon them.

You can read more about Campaigns and Promotions on page 23.

Campaigns, Promotions & Deals

NAME/DESCRIPTION: _____

DETAILS: _____

_____

RESULTS: _____

_____

_____

NAME/DESCRIPTION: _____

DETAILS: _____

_____

RESULTS: _____

_____

_____

NAME/DESCRIPTION: _____

DETAILS: _____

_____

RESULTS: _____

_____

_____

Campaigns, Promotions & Deals

NAME/DESCRIPTION: _____

DETAILS: _____

_____

RESULTS: _____

_____

_____

NAME/DESCRIPTION: _____

DETAILS: _____

_____

RESULTS: _____

_____

_____

NAME/DESCRIPTION: _____

DETAILS: _____

_____

RESULTS: _____

_____

_____

Campaigns, Promotions & Deals

NAME/DESCRIPTION:

DETAILS:

RESULTS:

NAME/DESCRIPTION:

DETAILS:

RESULTS:

NAME/DESCRIPTION:

DETAILS:

RESULTS:

Campaigns, Promotions & Deals

NAME/DESCRIPTION: _____

DETAILS: _____

_____

RESULTS: _____

_____

_____

NAME/DESCRIPTION: _____

DETAILS: _____

_____

RESULTS: _____

_____

_____

NAME/DESCRIPTION: _____

DETAILS: _____

_____

RESULTS: _____

_____

_____

Campaigns, Promotions & Deals

NAME/DESCRIPTION: _____

DETAILS: _____

_____

RESULTS: _____

_____

_____

NAME/DESCRIPTION: _____

DETAILS: _____

_____

RESULTS: _____

_____

_____

NAME/DESCRIPTION: _____

DETAILS: _____

_____

RESULTS: _____

_____

_____

CAMPAIGNS, PROMOTIONS & DEALS

NAME/DESCRIPTION:

DETAILS:

RESULTS:

NAME/DESCRIPTION:

DETAILS:

RESULTS:

NAME/DESCRIPTION:

DETAILS:

RESULTS:

Campaigns, Promotions & Deals

NAME/DESCRIPTION: _____

DETAILS: _____

_____

RESULTS: _____

_____

_____

NAME/DESCRIPTION: _____

DETAILS: _____

_____

RESULTS: _____

_____

_____

NAME/DESCRIPTION: _____

DETAILS: _____

_____

RESULTS: _____

_____

_____

Campaigns, Promotions & Deals

NAME/DESCRIPTION: _____

DETAILS: _____

_____

RESULTS: _____

_____

_____

NAME/DESCRIPTION: _____

DETAILS: _____

_____

RESULTS: _____

_____

_____

NAME/DESCRIPTION: _____

DETAILS: _____

_____

RESULTS: _____

_____

_____

CAMPAIGNS, PROMOTIONS & DEALS

NAME/DESCRIPTION: _____

DETAILS: _____

_____

RESULTS: _____

_____

_____

NAME/DESCRIPTION: _____

DETAILS: _____

_____

RESULTS: _____

_____

_____

NAME/DESCRIPTION: _____

DETAILS: _____

_____

RESULTS: _____

_____

_____

CAMPAIGNS, PROMOTIONS & DEALS

NAME/DESCRIPTION: _____

DETAILS: _____

_____

RESULTS: _____

_____

_____

NAME/DESCRIPTION: _____

DETAILS: _____

_____

RESULTS: _____

_____

_____

NAME/DESCRIPTION: _____

DETAILS: _____

_____

RESULTS: _____

_____

_____

Hotel Reputation Page

Maintaining a helicopter view of the entirety of your hotel's reputation and how it evolves over time is essential to your hotel's success. Like a helicopter flies high to see the landscape as a whole, as a hotel revenue manager you always want to be aware of your hotel's current guest satisfaction score and how it changes. Just as a helicopter can also swoop low to look more closely at something, you'll want to investigate the details *behind* your guest satisfaction score to understand what makes it higher or what drags it down.

Use this page to record your hotel's guest satisfaction score on a regular basis and to take notes on what influences it, how it compares to your competitors, and what steps you could take to raise it.

HOTEL REPUTATION

DATE	GUEST SATISFACTION SCORE	NOTES

HOTEL REPUTATION

DATE	GUEST SATISFACTION SCORE	NOTES

HOTEL REPUTATION

DATE	GUEST SATISFACTION SCORE	NOTES

HOTEL REPUTATION

DATE	GUEST SATISFACTION SCORE	NOTES

HOTEL REPUTATION

DATE	GUEST SATISFACTION SCORE	NOTES

Braindump

There are times when you need to jot something down that you absolutely cannot forget for later. Other times, a brilliant idea might strike that you need to spell out before your inspiration is lost. During times like these, having a Braindump will come in handy. Whether you need to sketch out a budget, brainstorm some long-term revenue goals, or take notes during a meeting, a Braindump allows you to commit your important thoughts to record.

BRAINDUMP

NOTES, IDEAS... ANYTHING

Glossary of Terms

Average Daily Rate (ADR) – A measure of the average room rate paid per rooms sold. To calculate ADR, divide room revenue by rooms sold.

Average Length of Stay (ALOS) – A measure of the total room nights in a hotel (or in a specific segment) per the number of total reservations in the hotel. To calculate ALOS, divide total occupied room nights by total bookings.

Average Rate Index (ARI) – A measure to determine whether the hotel realizes its fair share of ADR compared to a competitive set. To calculate ARI, divide the hotel's ADR by the ADR of a competitive set (that is representative of the market). An ARI equal to 1.00 indicates that the hotel has secured an equal share of revenue based on ADR compared to the competitive set. An ARI above 1.00 indicates a hotel has secured a greater share. An ARI below 1.00 indicates that the hotel has secured a lesser share. Multiply ARI by 100 or convert it to a percentage to ease the burden of working with this measurement.

Best Available Rate (BAR) – The lowest unqualified rate for a room type available to the general public. BAR provides a guarantee that guests will not find a lower rate for the same room type on a given night(s) on an OTA or elsewhere. This is also a common rate used for rate comparisons between hotels.

Block / Group pricing – A non-yieldable rate applied to a fixed number of rooms reserved for a specified group. A window exists during which members of the specified group must book their rooms in order to receive the non-yieldable rate.

Booking curve – A tool that can visually represent bookings over time, incorporating data such as pickup, number of bookings, availability and yielding capacity of the hotel.

Booking window or Booking lead time – The time period between when a hotel reservation is made and a guest's actual arrival date. Measures how far in advance rooms are booked.

Break-even – the point at which revenues equal costs.

Budget – Establishes a hotel's financial plan for the upcoming calendar or fiscal year. Generally, it should designate a daily occupancy, ADR and RevPAR for every major market segment. It outlines percentage changes over previous years, both by month and by quarter. This annual budget comprises part of the overall financial budget for the hotel.

Capacity – The number of rooms a hotel has to offer.

Central Reservation System (CRS) – A system to manage the booking process and existing reservations, and to maintain hotel information and data, including rates and inventory. Systems can either be created in-house or by a third-party vendor.

Channel management – The techniques and systems hotels use to update hotel information, room inventory and rates in each of their distribution channels.

Channels – The different means by which potential guests can reserve or book a hotel room.

Closed to arrival (CTA) – An inventory control mechanism used by revenue managers to prevent new reservations being made by guest arriving on a specific date. The only guests permitted to use such inventory are those arriving at earlier dates and remaining over the CTA date.

Cold / slow periods – A period of time (season, month, day, or time of day) when operating performance (demand) is low. Cold periods are times when revenue managers might discount rates or offer incentives in an attempt to increase occupancy and improve RevPAR.

Commission – The payment that a travel agent or other third party receives for each reservation made through their office or site.

Competitive set (or Compset) – Consists of a group of hotels recognized as direct competitors to the hotel by which the hotel can compare itself against the group's aggregate performance.

Conversion – The process of a guest moving from gathering information about a hotel or shopping for a room to taking action by making direct inquiries or finalizing a booking.

Conversion Rate (CR) – A statistical measure of the number of people who click an ad who eventually make a purchase associated with that ad. To calculate CR, divide the total number of buyers by the total number of unique clicks.

Cost Per Click (CPC) – The average cost to an advertiser incurred as a result of a consumer clicking an online ad.

Click Through Rate (CTR) – A measure of the total number of webpage impressions that result in clicks, representing the number of people who actually see an advertisement. To calculate CTR, divide the total number of clicks by the total number of unique impressions.

Demand – The amount of interest in a hotel, including in its beds, rooms, event spaces, etc.

Denial – A response to a potential guest's request stating that a hotel cannot accommodate any additional guests because it is fully booked or a restriction has been placed on the date requested.

Displacement Analysis – An analysis conducted to determine whether it's prudent to take rooms out of a hotel's inventory— usually to accommodate a group's request—that could be requested later at a higher rate by late-booking or walk-in guests. To conduct a displacement analysis, multiply the number of rooms denied by the average rate for that segment of business. If the resulting number is higher than the group revenue, then the group's request should be denied.

Dynamic pricing – A method hotels employ to help optimize profitability by changing prices for a room or service in response to changes in capacity, competition, demand and other guest attributes.

Elastic demand – When consumer demand responds to price changes. Factors that can influence elastic demand include increased competition, standardized services and perceived luxury.

Fenced rate – A rate that offers benefits to potential guests, but with conditions or requirements that apply in order to secure a reservation. To procure such a rate, reservations are often nonrefundable, purchased in advance and cannot be canceled.

Fixed pricing – A pricing strategy in which prices do not fluctuate based on demand, product characteristics or segmentation within markets.

Forecast – A prediction of the number of rooms that can be sold on a specific date or period of time. Accurate forecasting greatly enhances other revenue management strategies according to the expected level of demand.

Generic search – A search for a product in which the user does not enter a brand name as a keyword. When searching for a hotel, a user might type "downtown hotels in Boston," when seeking information about hotels in the Boston area, rather than specify a known hotel or chain.

Global Distribution Systems (GDS) – Four of the most recognized reservation systems in the industry: Amadeus, Galileo, Sabre and Worldspan.

Gross Operating Profit Per Available Room (GOPPAR) – A measure of total revenue less operational and marketing expenses per room used to measure a hotel's performance and to make adjustments accordingly. To calculate GOPPAR, subtract operational/marketing expenses per room from the total revenue brought in by rooms sold.

Group Displacement – A process of measuring a group's total profitability compared to the profitability of gaining business from other channels that would otherwise be displaced by the group.

Group forecasting – Making educated estimates for how many group block rooms will be booked and when, based on previous booking data.

Group Pricing – *See Block / Group Pricing*

Group segment mix – The proportions of the different group segments that comprise the total group business for the hotel. In general, these segments receive different rates.

Inelastic demand – When consumer demand does not respond to prices changes. Factors that can influence inelastic demand are reduced competition, differentiated services and consumer staples.

Landing page – The "front page" of a site a web user first arrives at as a result of clicking on a listing's link in a search.

Last room availability clause (LRA) – A contract clause—often agreed upon between the hotel and third-party agents—indicating that the contracted rate is available as long as rooms of any type remain available.

Leisure traveler – A traveler who travels for personal reasons rather than for work. Leisure travelers are not business travelers.

Length of stay – The number of nights a guest has booked at the hotel.

Length-of-stay controls – Controls put in place to help regulate demand for rooms in an effort to organize and optimize occupancy for a hotel.

Market Penetration Index (MPI) – A measure to help the hotel recognize its position in proportion to its competition by determining whether the hotel realizes its fair share of occupancy. To calculate MPI, divide the occupancy percentage of the hotel by the occupancy percentage of the competitive set (that is representative of the market). An MPI equal to 1.00 indicates that the hotel has secured an equal share of occupancy compared to the competitive set. An MPI above 1.00 indicates a hotel has secured a greater share of occupancy. An MPI below 1.00 indicates that the hotel has secured a lesser share of occupancy. Multiply MPI by 100 or convert it to a percentage to ease the burden of working with this measurement.

Metasearch engine – A website that can search all OTAs on behalf of a consumer and display the best available prices based on predefined criteria.

Net rate – The sell rate with commissions sometimes required by third-parties (namely, OTAs) already subtracted.

Occupancy – A measure of the percentage of available rooms sold during a specific period of time. To calculate occupancy, divide the number of rooms sold by rooms available.

Occupancy Index – A measure of the hotel's occupancy percentage compared to the occupancy percentage of the competitive set (that is representative of the market). To calculate the occupancy index, divide the hotel occupancy percentage by the occupancy percentage of the competitive set, then multiply by 100.

Online Travel Agency (OTA) – A web-based hotel and travel reservations system. Hotels offer inventory to OTAs, which sell rooms in exchange for a commission.

Opaque – Describes a booking channel that shields the identity of a hotel until a guest completes their reservation. It can also describe channels where guests must first become members to gain access to special rates.

Overbooking – A tactic of booking reservations beyond capacity to offset cancelled reservations and no-shows.

Pace – *See Pickup*

Pay Per Click (PPC) – An Internet advertising model where advertisers use ad links to direct traffic from host websites to their own websites or products. Advertisers pay the owners of host websites a fee each time an ad of theirs is clicked.

Perishable inventory – Inventory, that if not used within a specific period of time, becomes a lost revenue opportunity. A hotel room is perishable inventory.

Pickup / Pace – The rate at which reservations are booked for a specific date.

Price Elasticity – A measure showing how demand for a room responds to a change in its price.

Property Management System (PMS) – A hotel's onsite system that facilitates management processes for the hotel, including guest check-in and check-out.

Rate parity – A guarantee that potential guests will be quoted the same price for the same product regardless of where they shop. It allows individual hotels and chains to set the same price for each of their room types across all distribution channels.

Reference price – The price consumers think a service, product or room should cost. Points of reference for prices include the price last paid, the price most frequently paid, the price other consumers have paid for the same thing, or market prices and posted prices.

Regression – A statistical analysis for evaluating the relationships that exist among variables. It measures the association between one variable (the dependent variable) and one or more other variables (the independent variables), usually formulated in an equation.

Reputation management – Influencing and controlling an individual's or business's reputation, particularly as it appears online or through social media.

Revenue Generating Index (RGI) – *See RevPAR Index (RPI)*

Revenue Management – The art and science of predicting real-time customer demand and optimizing the price and availability of products to match that demand.

RevPAR Index (RPI) – A measure to determine whether the hotel realizes its fair share of revenue compared to a competitive set. To calculate RPI, divide the RevPAR of the hotel by the RevPAR of the competitive set (that is representative of the market). An RPI equal to 1.00 indicates that the hotel has secured its fair share of revenue compared to hotels it the competitive set. An RPI above 1.00 indicates the hotel has secured a greater share. An RPI below 1.00 indicates that the hotel has secured a lesser share. Multiply RPI by 100 or convert it to a percentage to ease the burden of working with this measurement.

RevPATI – Revenue per available time-based inventory unit. RevPAR and RevPASH are variations on this measure. RevPATI is calculated differently depending on the context. It is used in all applications of revenue management to analyze a hotel's or chain's ability to optimize its revenue capacity.

Revenue per available room (RevPAR) – A measure of how well a hotel manages its inventory and rates in order to optimize revenue. To calculate, multiply occupancy by ADR.

Search engine optimization (SEO) – The process of maximizing unique visitors to a website by improving the site's position in organic search results.

Segmented markets – Markets composed of consumers bearing similar characteristics. Segments can be comprised based on consumers' ages, purchasing power, frequency of purchase, and affiliation to groups; or be differentiated by how much they are willing to pay for a service, product or room.

Shoulder Date – Dates that fall directly beside or very close to other high demand dates. A Friday and a Sunday are each considered shoulder dates when they are not sold out, but the Saturday between them is.

Stay Pattern Management – The process or optimizing hotel capacity by ensuring the stay patterns on the books do not result in unsellable stay patterns remaining to be booked.

Time-variable demand – Uncertain demand that varies by time of year, day of week, in relation to holidays, etc.

Transient – Non-group or non-committed business (guests). These guests are largely on-the-move and seeking short stays.

Unconstrained Demand – A forecast of the quantity of rooms a hotel could sell if had an unlimited number of rooms—that is, no constraints or limits.

Variable pricing – Simultaneously offering varying prices at different points-of-sale (including websites) for the same service, product or room.

Wash – The fraction of the group block that the group does not utilize.

Win rates – The rate at which potential guests accept offers.

Worldspan – GDS system originally designed for airlines, now widely used by travel agents to book all forms of travel.

Yield – Revenue made. Includes the dynamic pricing, overbooking and allocation of perishable assets necessary to maximize revenue.

Yield Management – Synonymous with Revenue Management, the purpose of Yield Management is to maximize revenue and profits. The process involves understanding, anticipating and reacting to guests' needs and behavior, with the intention of increasing yield.